TANGRAM ALPHABET

BUILDING LETTERS WITH TANGRAMS

by

Anne Linehan and Janis Poe

Published by
Teaching Resource Center
P.O. Box 82777
San Diego, CA 92138

Edited by Laura Woodard
Illustrations by Linda Starr

©1999 Teaching Resource Center
All Rights Reserved.
Permission is granted to individual classroom teachers to
reproduce portions of this book for classroom use only.

PRINTED IN THE UNITED STATES OF AMERICA
ISBN: 1-56785-045-6

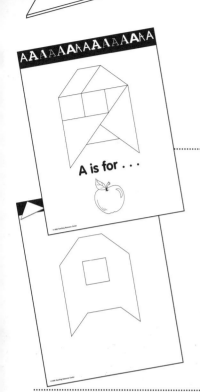

Tangrams are popular manipulatives that provide problem solving experiences for students of all ages. The tangram puzzle has seven pieces that make up a square. The pieces are called tans.

Tangrams are used for creating shapes, storytelling and investigating mathematics. In this book children will use the tangrams to cover letters of the alphabet. Each letter puzzle is shown twice.

The first puzzle provides a beginning experience and includes the outline of each of the tangram pieces. Children must slide, turn and flip the pieces in order for them to fit within the outline.

The second is a challenge puzzle. There are no shape outlines within the puzzle, only the outline of the letter.

GETTING STARTED

- One tangram set of seven pieces is needed to cover each letter.
- Copy the letters that include the shape outlines onto sturdy paper.
- Set up classroom management rules, and make sure the children understand the proper handling of tangrams. Then have them spend time freely exploring with the tangrams.

PROCEDURE

- Have the children help you cover a letter puzzle with the tangrams.
- Have each child choose the letter for his or her name. It may be necessary to make multiple copies of the letters.
- Set up a center where children can explore with the tangrams. Make sure they have easy access to the letter puzzles. Encourage them to explore all the letters of the alphabet.

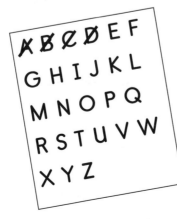

Provide the students with a way of keeping track of the letters they have already tested.

NEXT STEPS

- Ask the children to create pictures with the tangrams. Have them trace around the pieces and create new puzzles for their classmates.
- Have the children use the seven pieces to make a square.
- Read *Grandfather Tang's Story* by Ann Tompert (Crown Publishers, 1990). This story is told with tangrams.
- Write classroom books that are full of tangram characters.

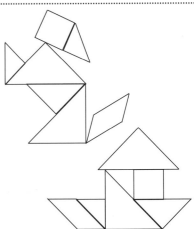

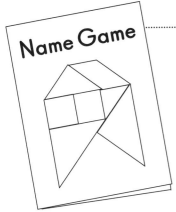

Make a book patterned after the name game rhyme. Have the children create tangram alphabets by gluing paper tangrams on letter puzzles. Then each child can fill in a sentence frame based on the rhyme.

A my name is ___Alice___ and my friend's name is ___Abel___.

We come from ___Alabama___ and we like ___alligators___.

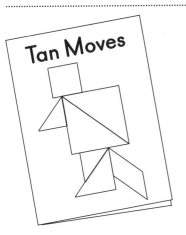

Make a book that will help children discuss **verbs** in a meaningful context.
- Have each child create a "Tan" figure that looks like someone jumping, kicking, stretching, running, dancing or twisting.
- Have the class brainstorm a name for the book.
- Have each child write about the Tan figure they created. For beginning level writing, use a sentence frame.

What do you think Tan wants to do?

Tan wants to _____.

Possible ending phrases:
**run like the wind.
stretch to the sky.
glide on ice.
dive into the sea.
dance on the stage.
jump for joy.**

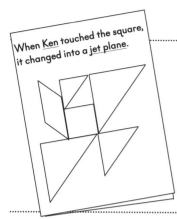

When <u>Ken</u> touched the square, it changed into a <u>jet plane</u>.

Make a book that will help children discuss **nouns** in a meaningful context. Provide a sentence frame:

When ＿＿＿＿＿ touched the square it changed

into a ＿＿＿＿ .

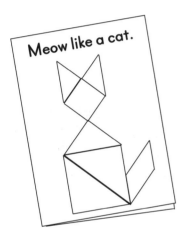

Meow like a cat.

Make a science book about animals and their sounds. Have the children make tangram animals. Discuss and research each type of animal; include the sounds and actions each animal makes. Have each child write about the tan animal they created. You may want to provide a sentence frame:

＿＿＿＿＿ like a ＿＿＿＿＿ .

Examples: **Roar like a lion.**
Peck like a bird.
Float like a whale.
Hop like a rabbit.
Meow like a cat.
Soar like an eagle.

RESOURCES

Tangrams:

Presto Chango!
by Anne Linehan (grades K-5)
Student story telling, classbook making and problem solving with tangrams.

Grandfather Tang's Story

Transparent Tangrams

Tangram Paper Shapes

Tangram Tracers

Letter Formation:

Blacklines for Letter Formation

Trace 'n Erase

Tactile Letters

Wikki Stix

Alphabet Linking Tent

All the above are available from Teaching Resource Center • 1-800-833-3389 • www.trcabc.com

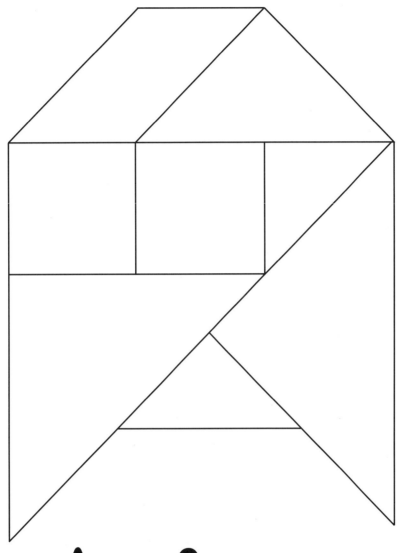

A is for . . .

©1999 Teaching Resource Center

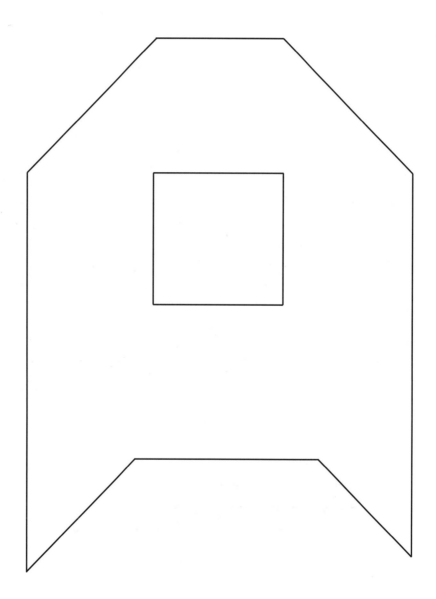

©1999 Teaching Resource Center

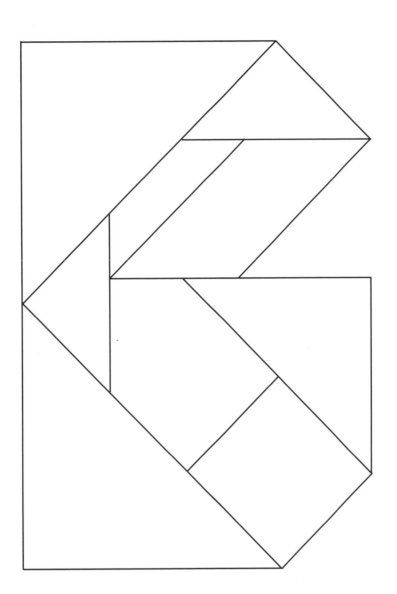

B is for . . .

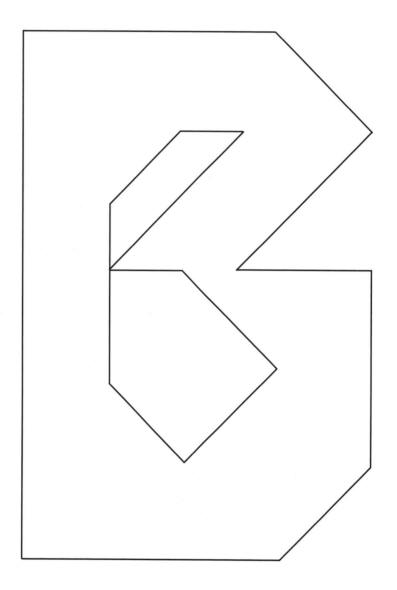

©1999 Teaching Resource Center

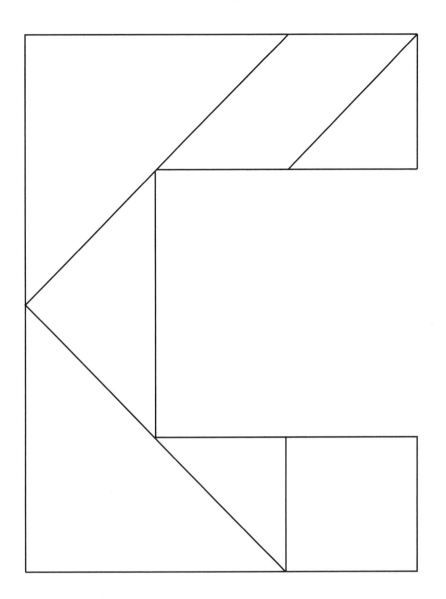

C is for . . .

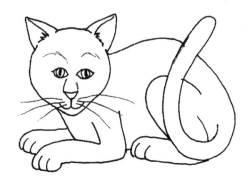

©1999 Teaching Resource Center

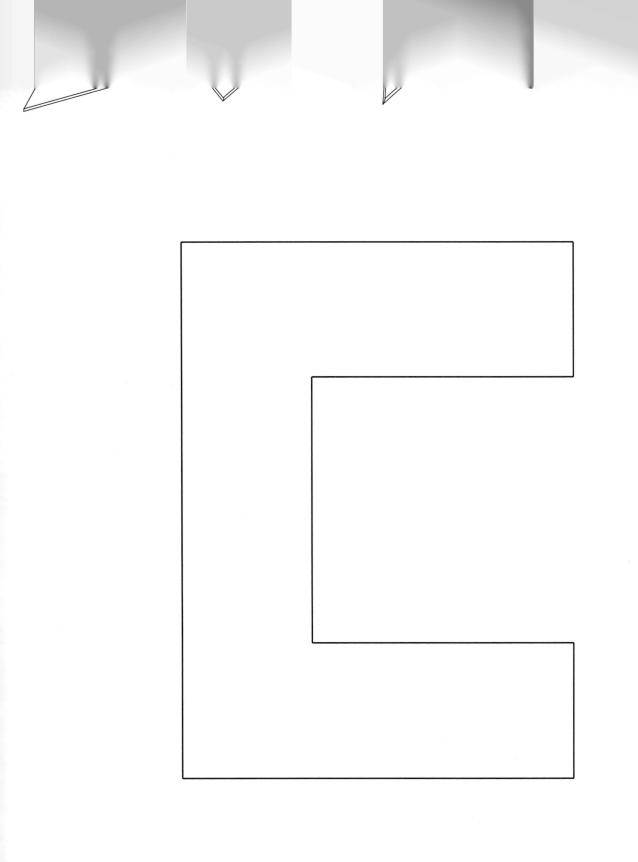

©1999 Teaching Resource Center

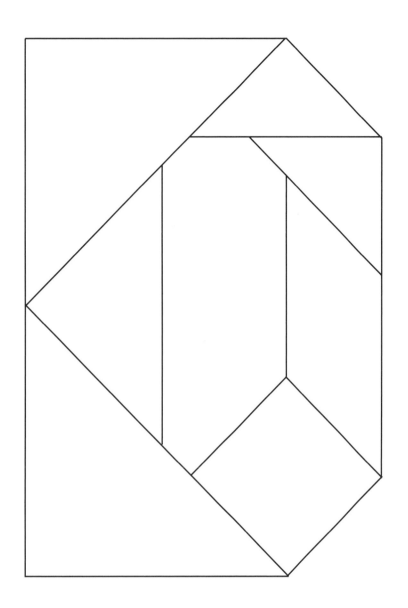

D is for . . .

©1999 Teaching Resource Center

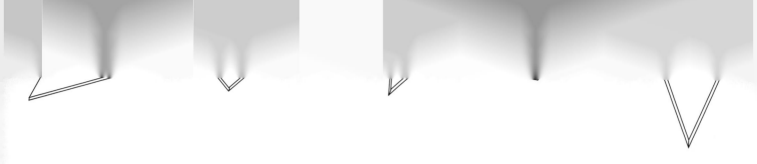

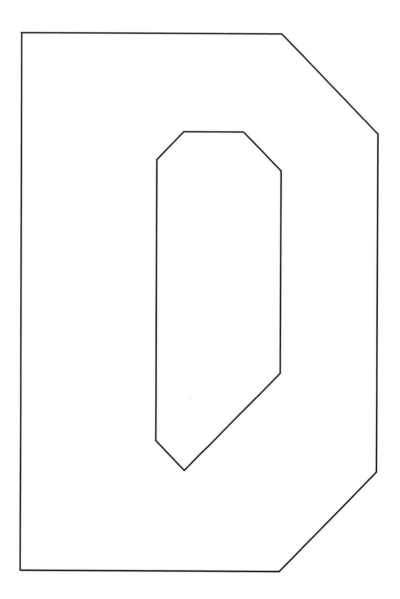

©1999 Teaching Resource Center

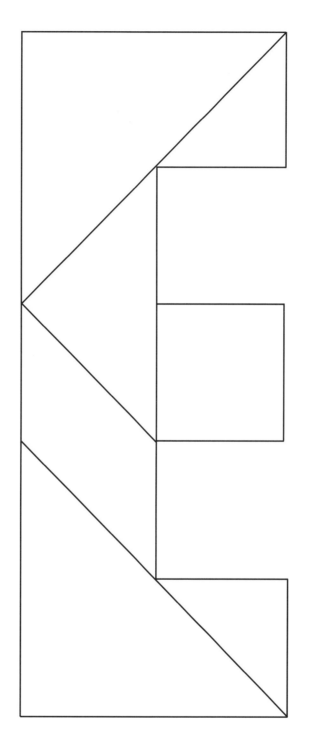

E is for . . .

©1999 Teaching Resource Center

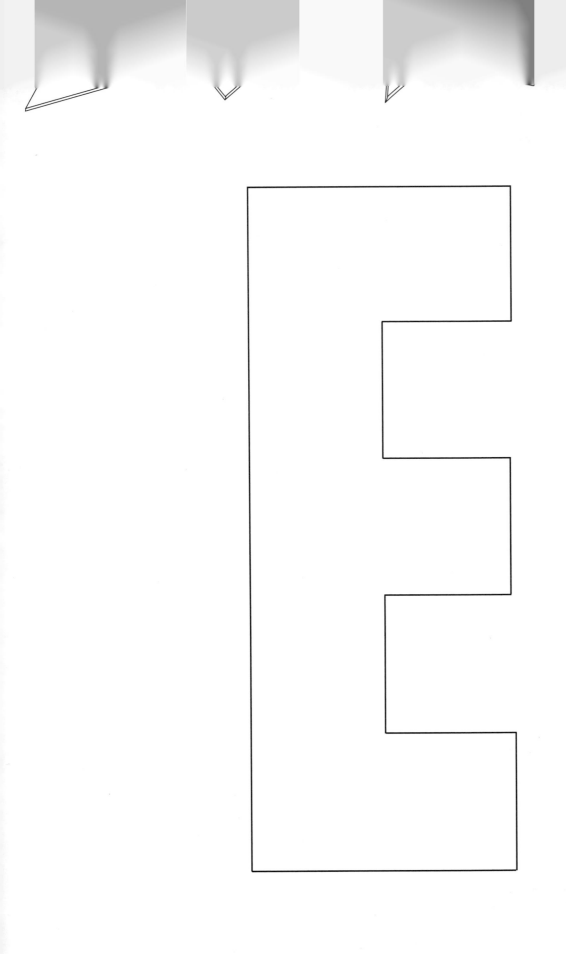

©1999 Teaching Resource Center

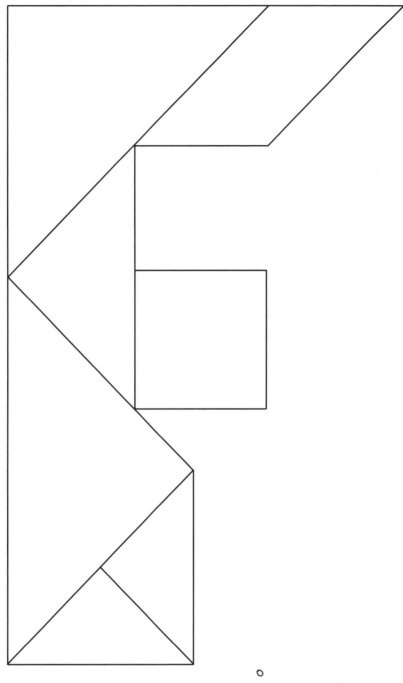

F is for . . .

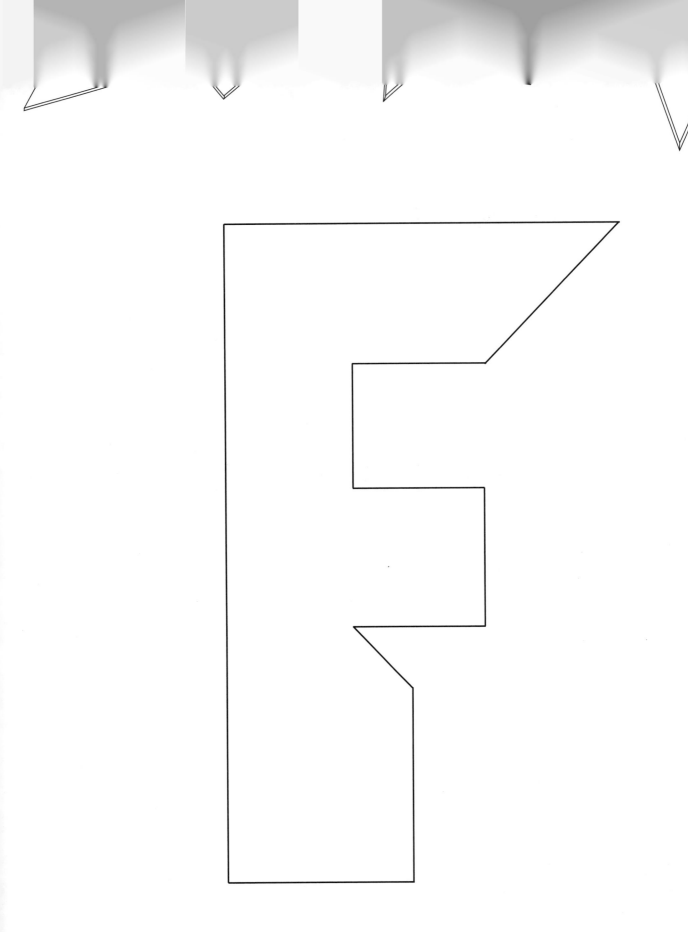

©1999 Teaching Resource Center

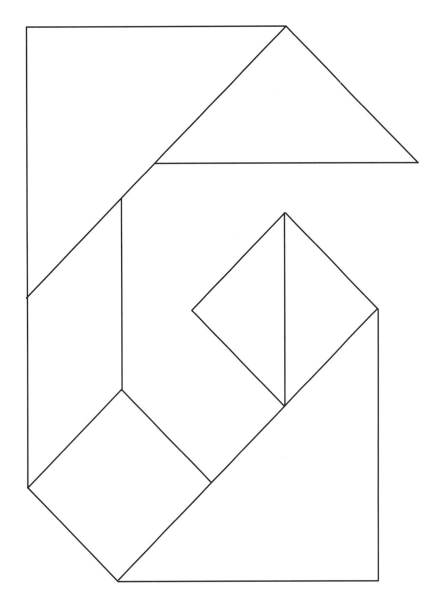

G is for . . .

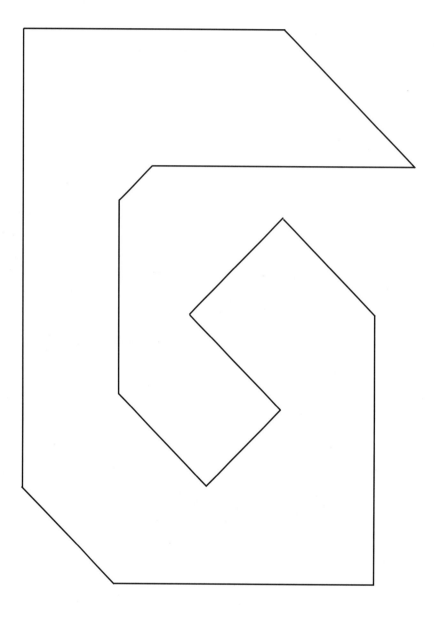

©1999 Teaching Resource Center

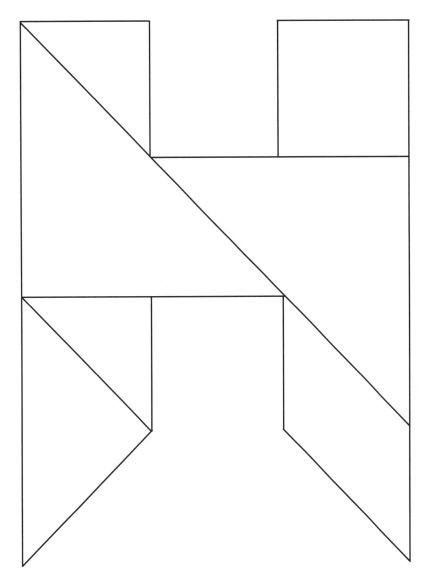

H is for . . .

©1999 Teaching Resource Center

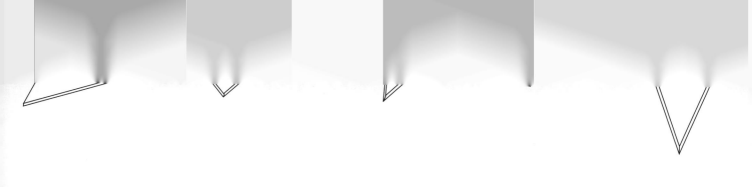

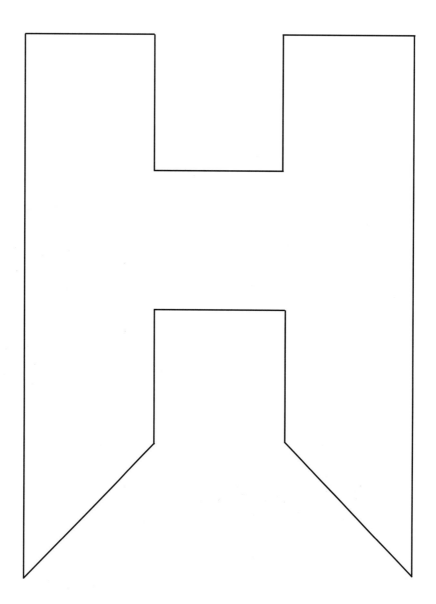

©1999 Teaching Resource Center

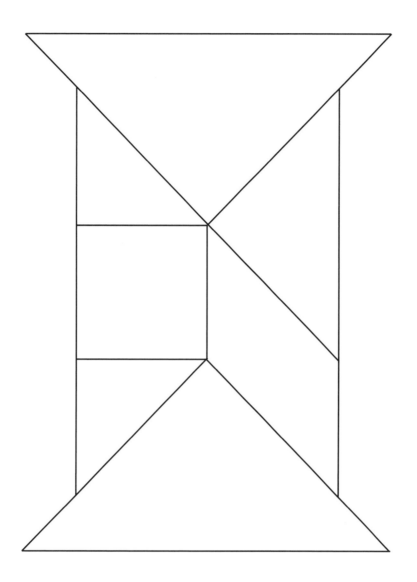

I is for . . .

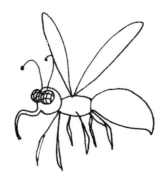

©1999 Teaching Resource Center

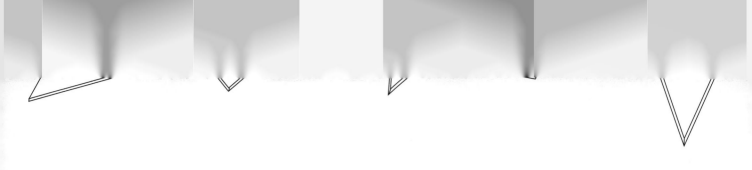

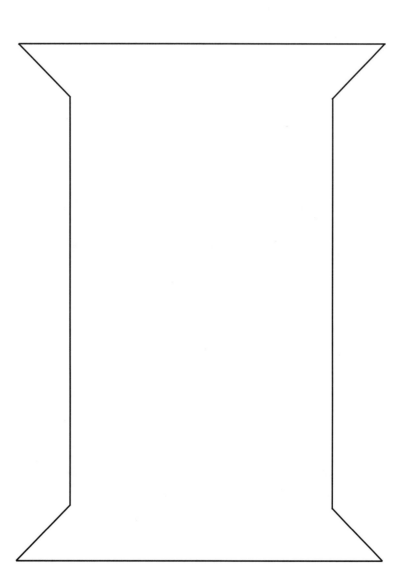

©1999 Teaching Resource Center

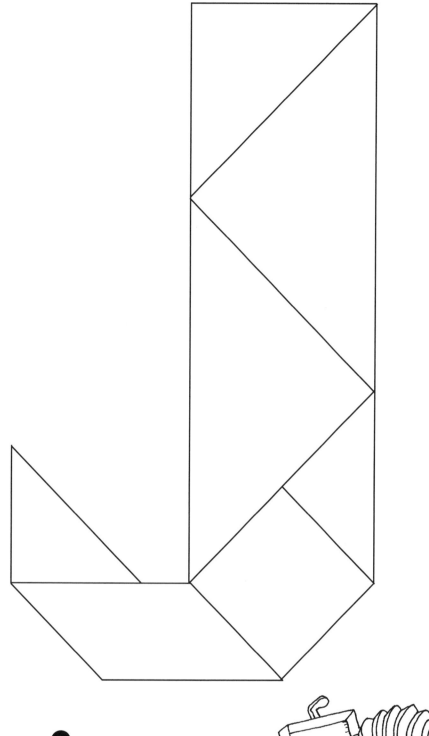

J is for . . .

©1999 Teaching Resource Center

©1999 Teaching Resource Center

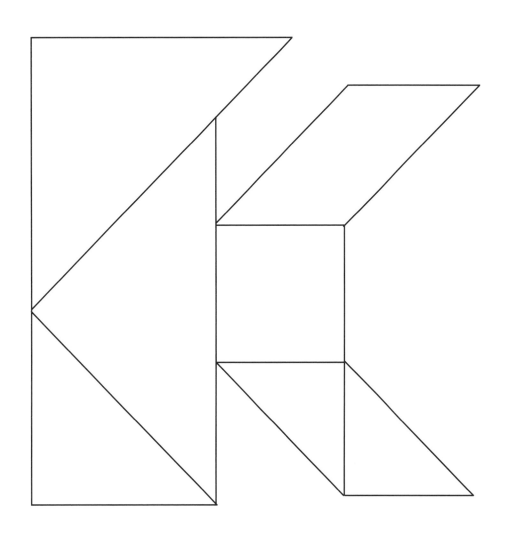

K is for . . .

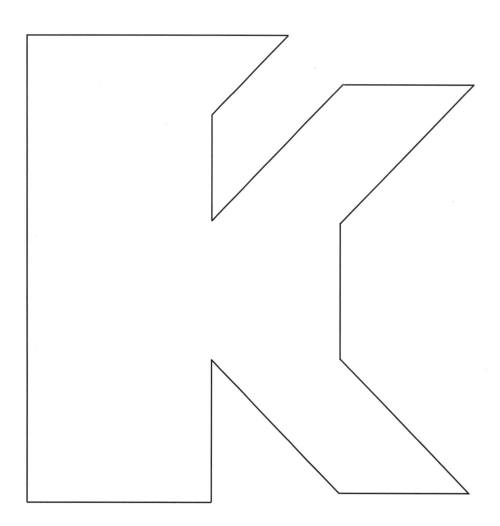

©1999 Teaching Resource Center

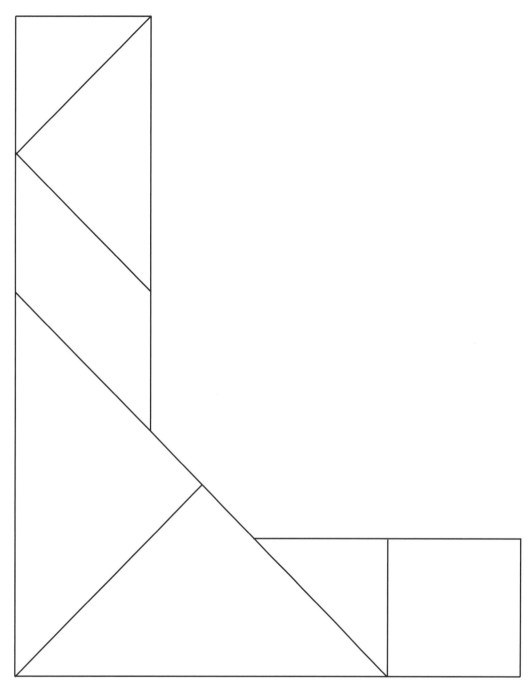

L is for . . .

©1999 Teaching Resource Center

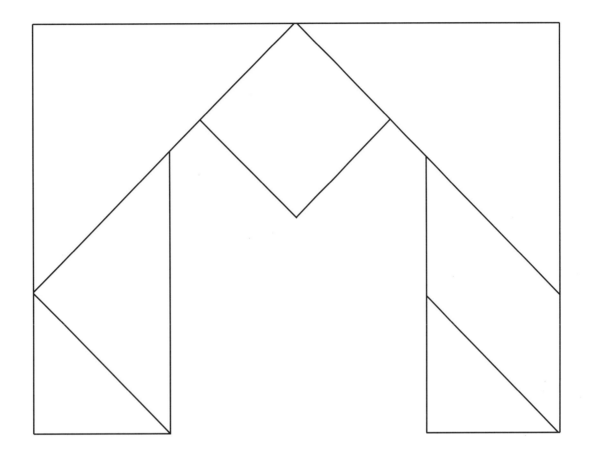

M is for . . .

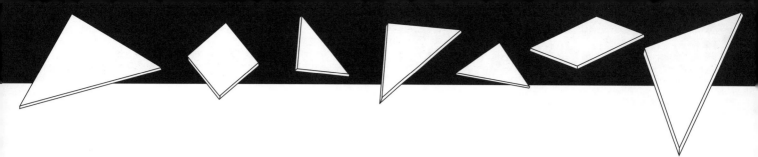

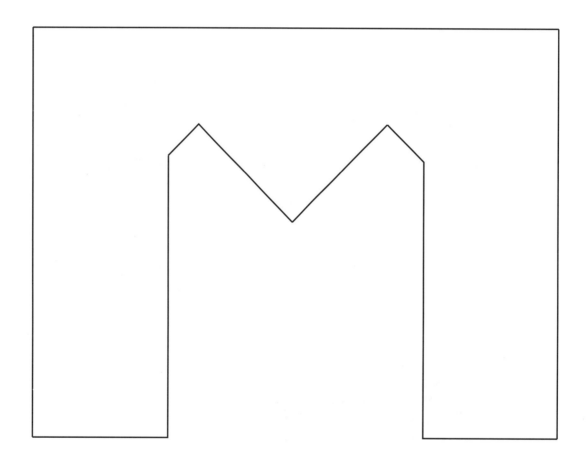

©1999 Teaching Resource Center

N is for . . .

©1999 Teaching Resource Center

©1999 Teaching Resource Center

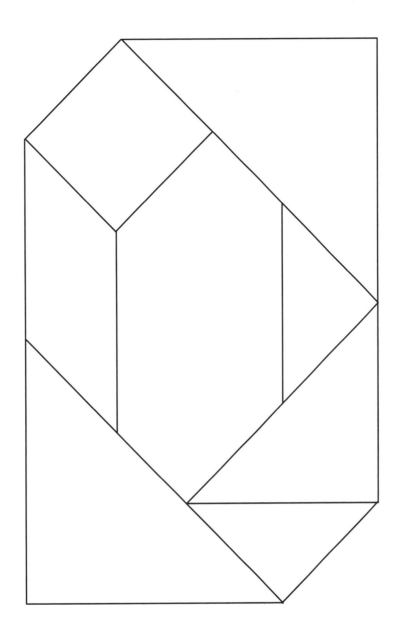

O is for . . .

©1999 Teaching Resource Center

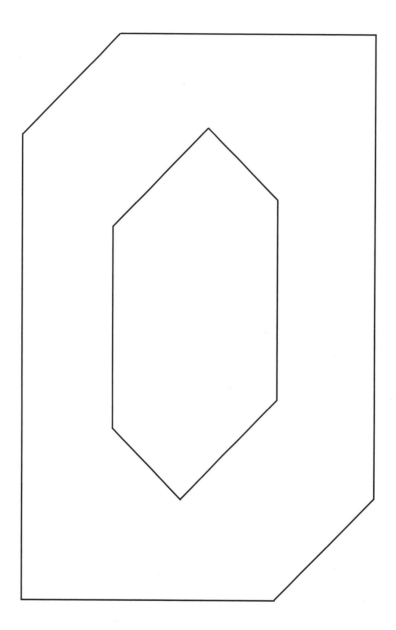

©1999 Teaching Resource Center

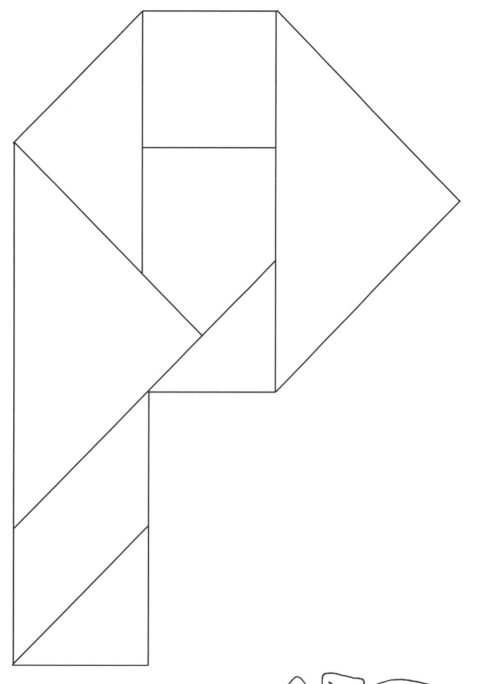

P is for . . .

©1999 Teaching Resource Center

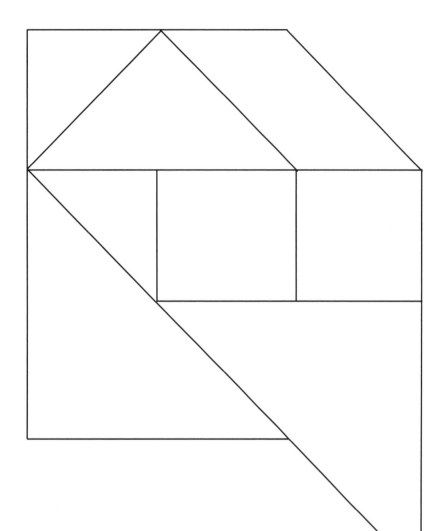

Q is for . . .

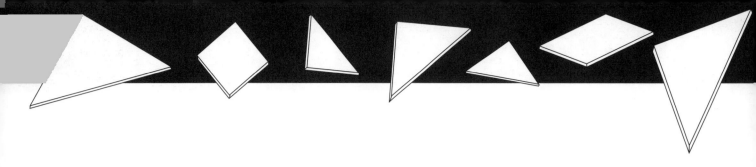

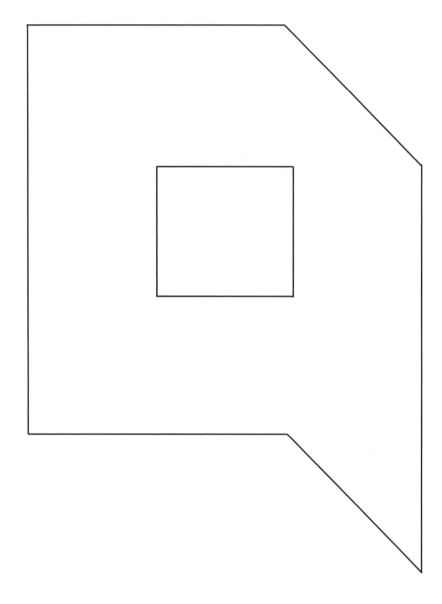

©1999 Teaching Resource Center

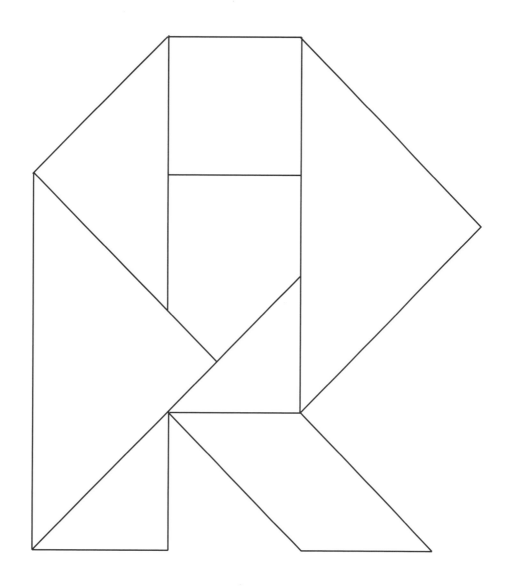

R is for . . .

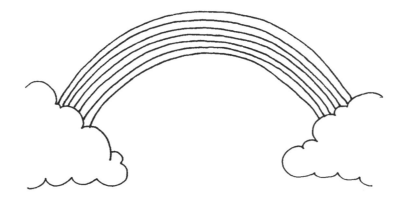

©1999 Teaching Resource Center

©1999 Teaching Resource Center

S is for . . .

©1999 Teaching Resource Center

©1999 Teaching Resource Center

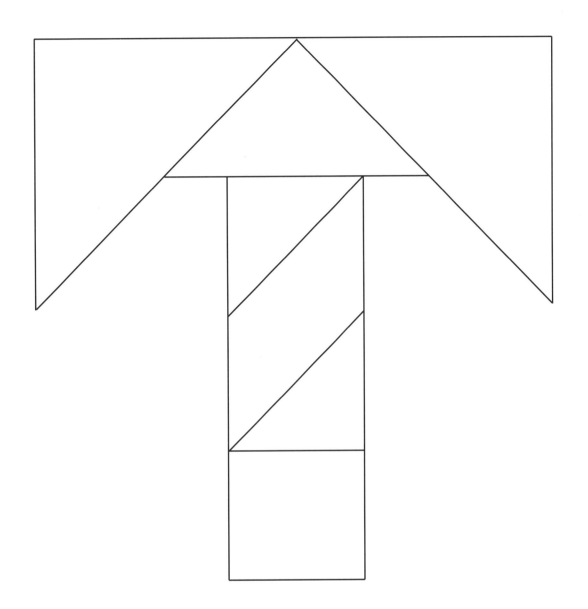

T is for . . .

©1999 Teaching Resource Center

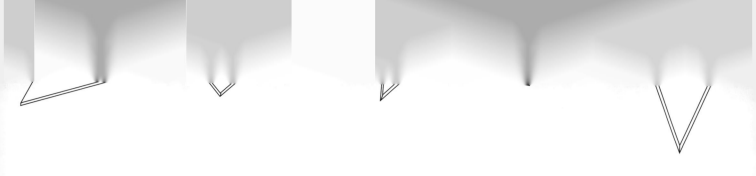

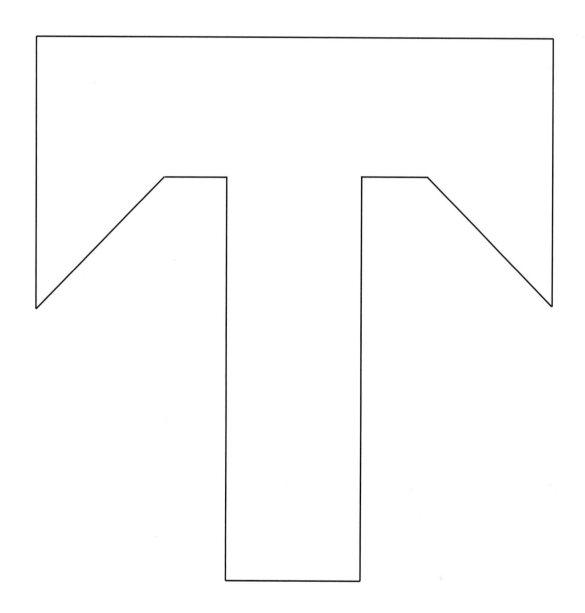

©1999 Teaching Resource Center

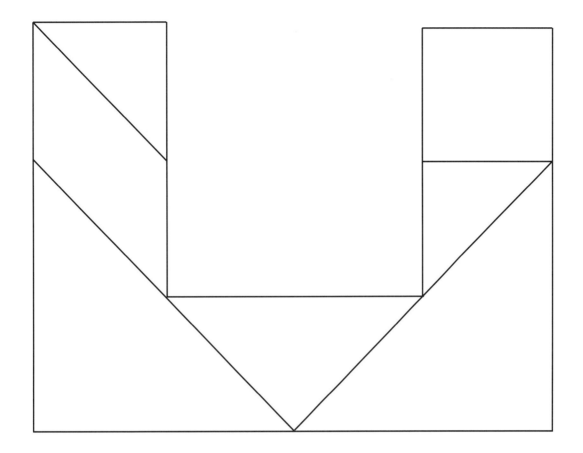

U is for . . .

©1999 Teaching Resource Center

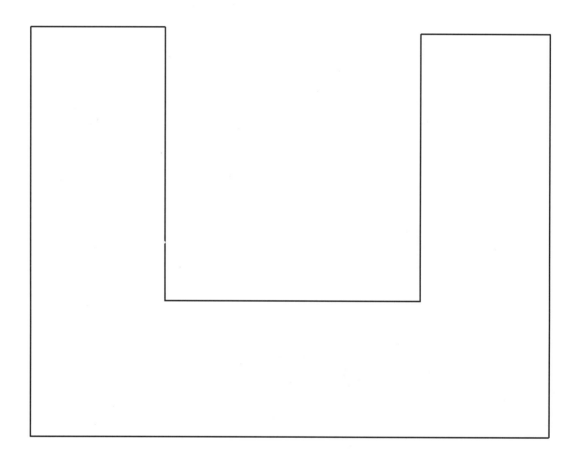

©1999 Teaching Resource Center

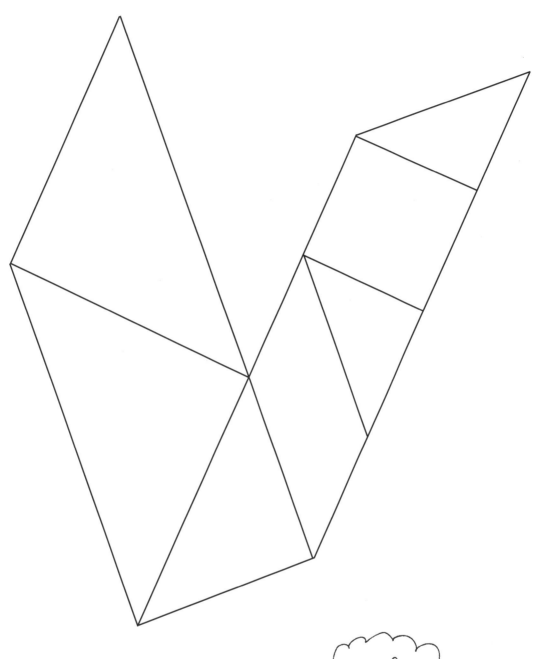

V is for . . .

©1999 Teaching Resource Center

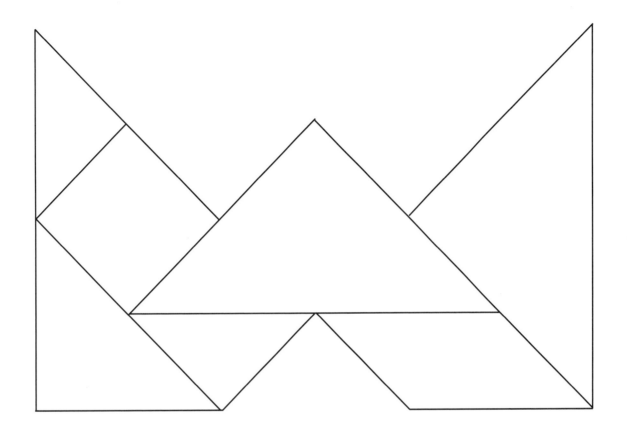

W is for . . .

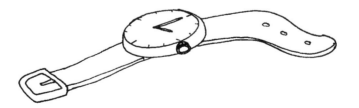

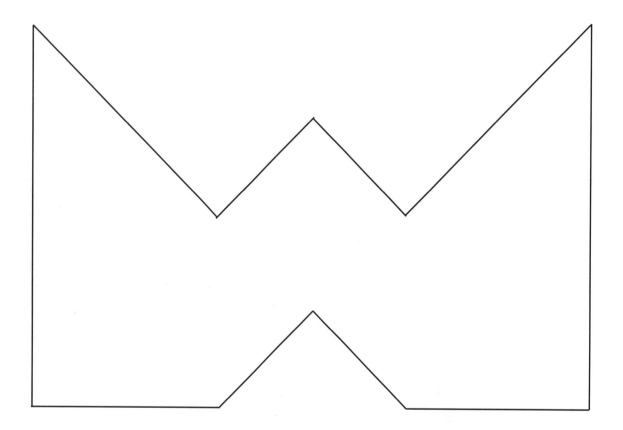

©1999 Teaching Resource Center

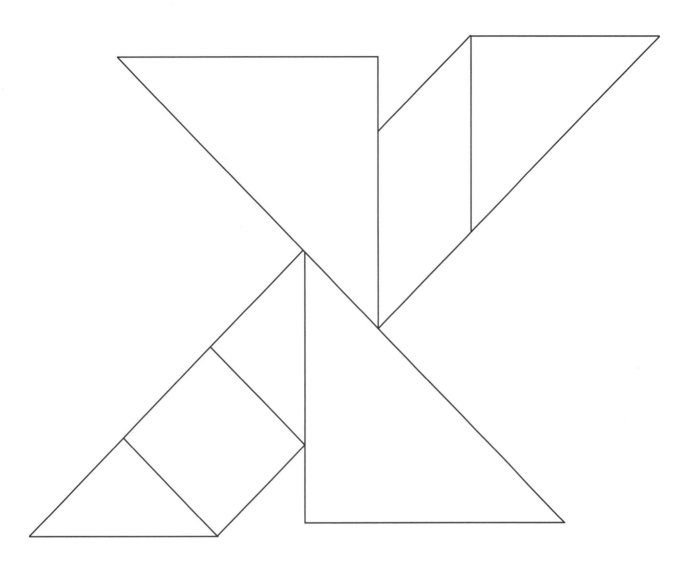

X is for . . .

©1999 Teaching Resource Center

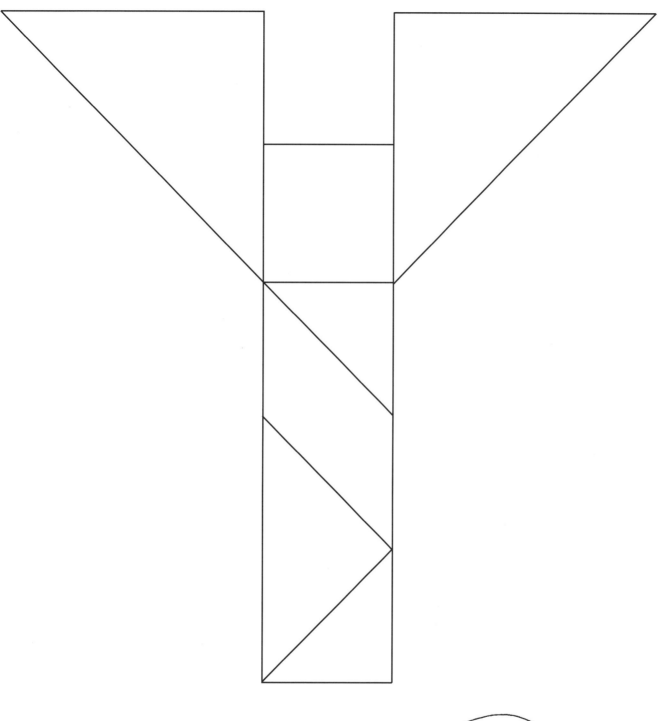

Y is for . . .

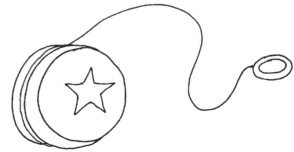

©1999 Teaching Resource Center

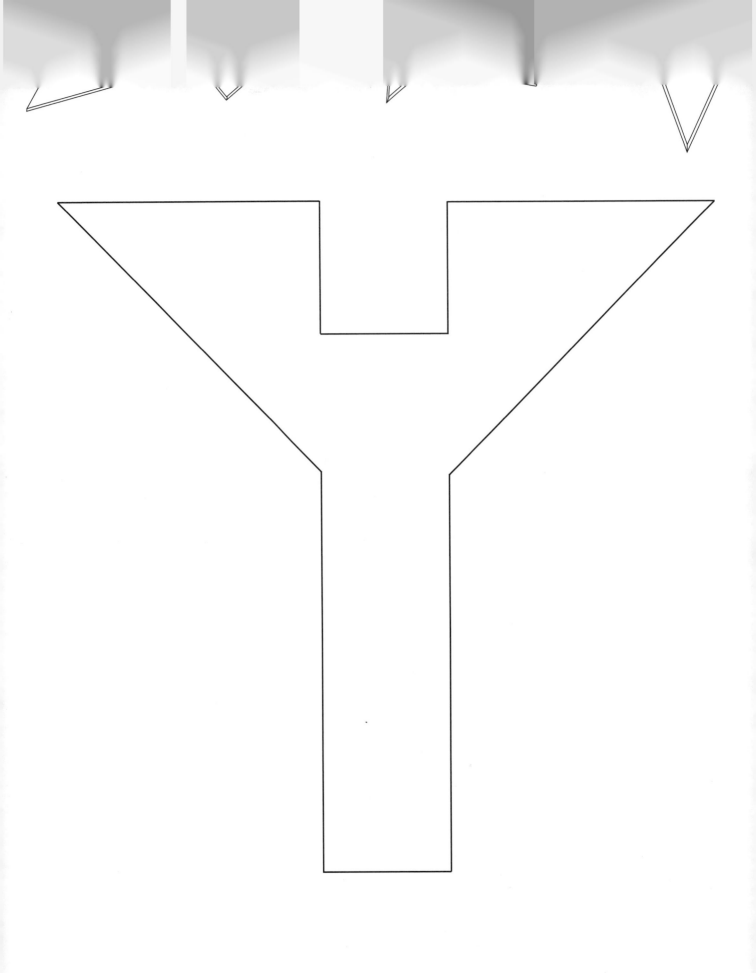

©1999 Teaching Resource Center

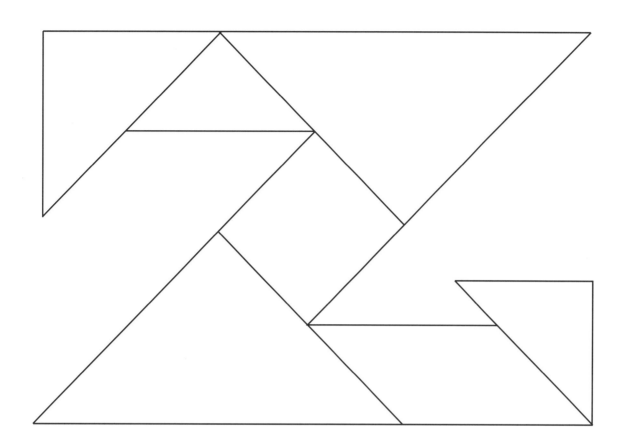

Z is for . . .

©1999 Teaching Resource Center

©1999 Teaching Resource Center